The Philosophical

Cul-de-sac

Tom Klehm

dedicated to lost souls

PREFACE

cul-de-sac ('kəl-di-ˌsak), n. a street
or passage closed at one end.

I have been cultivating this philosophy for
many years. Although it stands alone, those
familiar with Zen, Taoism and Satanism may
recognize familiar concepts. This philosophy
provides a singular unifying perspective of
reality. It is a perspective that has given me
absolute peace and equanimity. This book
contains a summary of this philosophy broken
into a series of declarations and imperatives.
Once this paradigm is successfully seen, it is
impossible to unsee. After internalizing it, you
may also find yourself in this elusive
metaphorical place which I have coined the
Philosophical Cul-de-sac.

This is a short book. That is by design. Numerous words are not required. This book can be approached in different ways. It can be digested in 20 minutes, 20 days or 20 years. That is up to you. To extract an overview of the philosophy, one may opt to read it straight through without pause. In order to fully benefit from it, one should meditate upon each statement. While meditating, consider the following. If you disagree with any statement, ask yourself why. Explore your arguments with an open mind. If you find yourself agreeing, explore the reasons why you agree. Spark a conversation. Explore with a friend. Dig deep. The intent of this book is not to change minds, but to open them. It is not meant to indoctrinate, but to liberate.

You are in prison and you don't even know it.

Escape.

Tom Klehm

You are an intelligent animal.

You have inherited a mind.

Your mind is powerful.

Your mind is an asset.

Your mind is your enemy.

Your mind can help you.

Your mind can hurt you.

Take control of your mind.

Know what is real.

Know what is not real.

Sight is real.

Hearing is real.

Smell is real.

Taste is real.

Touch is real.

This moment is real.

All else is an illusion.

Illusions do not exist.

Illusions only exist in your mind.

Thoughts are an illusion.

Ideas are an illusion.

.

Concepts are an illusion.

Memories are an illusion.

Dreams are an illusion.

Expectations are an illusion.

Regrets are an illusion.

Ambitions are an illusion.

Goals are an illusion.

Fears are an illusion.

Anxieties are an illusion.

Beliefs are an illusion.

Identity is an illusion.

Beauty is an illusion.

Success is an illusion.

Failure is an illusion.

Romance is an illusion.

Nostalgia is an illusion.

Sentiment is an illusion.

Value is an illusion.

Legacy is an illusion.

Reputation is an illusion.

Authority is an illusion.

Justice is an illusion.

Politics is an illusion.

Patriotism is an illusion.

Ideology is an illusion.

Religion is an illusion.

Spirituality is an illusion.

Karma is an illusion.

Enlightenment is an illusion.

Holiness is an illusion.

Morality is an illusion.

Sin is an illusion.

Heaven is an illusion.

Hell is an illusion.

Nirvana is an illusion.

Reincarnation is an illusion.

Afterlife is an illusion.

God is an illusion.

Your illusions distort what is real.

Your illusions imprison you.

You have been taught illusions.

You have created illusions.

Your instincts create illusions.

Desire for food is an instinct.

Desire for security is an instinct.

Desire for sex is an instinct.

Desire for acceptance is an instinct.

Desire for community is an instinct.

Recognize your instincts.

Recognize the illusions
created by your instincts.

Take control of your illusions.

Embrace the illusions that help you.

Discard the illusions that harm you.

Illusions can help you survive.

Illusions can help you thrive.

Illusions can bring you joy.

Illusions can depress you.

Illusions can enslave you.

Illusions can destroy you.

Illusions are not real.

Illusions are only tools.

Illusions are hollow.

Illusions are meaningless.

Meaning is only a product
of your mind.

The words you are reading
are only lines on a page.

Your mind gives the words meaning.

Meaning is an illusion.

Meaning is a prison.

Dogs bark.

Roosters crow.

Humans muse.

The mind never stops.

The mind is insatiable.

Desire for meaning is only an instinct.

Resist this instinct.

There is no meaning.

Life is meaningless.

Meaninglessness is liberation.

Meaninglessness is power.

Embrace meaninglessness.

Life has no purpose beyond
the context of survival.

Musings beyond the context
of survival are trivial.

Life is a game.

Life has no rules.

You make the rules.

You control meaning.

You control purpose.

Life is like a dream.

Turn life into a lucid dream.

Life is a river.

Flow with the river.

Flow against the river.

Decide how you will play.

Play as you choose.

There is no missing out.

Nothing is missed.

There is no waste of time.

Nothing is wasted.

There is no success.

There is no failure.

There is no good.

There is no bad.

All things are equal.

Nothing matters.

Stop caring.

Play the game.

"To seek is to suffer. To seek nothing is bliss."

Bodhidharma

POSTFACE

Yes, Marsianism is also an illusion,
albeit one of my favorites.

www.ingramcontent.com/pod-product-compliance
Lightning Source LLC
Chambersburg PA
CBHW060509030426
42337CB00015B/1816